"God, Can You Hear My Non-Speaking Voice?"

A Special Needs Child's Silent Prayer

By

Christine Goulbourne

Copyright © 2020 By Christine Goulbourne

All rights are reserved. No part of this book may be reproduced in whole or in part by any means of electronic or mechanical transmission, including copying, recording, or by any information storage or retrieval system without written permission from the publisher.

Illustrations by: Saluka Lakshith Perera

Published by Evershine Press, Inc.
1971 W Lumsden Rd #209
Brandon, FL 33511

Published in the United States of America

ISBN: 978-1-7364040-4-1 Paper

ISBN: 978-1-7364040-5-8 Hardback

Dedication

"I can do all things through Christ who strengthens me"

Philippians 4:13

I dedicate this book first to the Lord almighty, who in His infinite wisdom gave me this story idea.

To all special needs families everywhere, whether you go to church or not, God Hears you, Loves you, and He is always with you.

I thank my mom whose love is unwavering, my brother who is my comic relief, my husband who has been my strongest source of support with his love and fierce strength, my children Samantha, Tiki, and my son Richie who is brilliant and inspired this book.

I love my family and their incessant distractions; without them this book might have been published years ago.

This Book Belongs To

Each night after my mom tucks me into bed, she kisses me gently on the forehead and says, "It's time to pray my love."

She folds her hands and she prays:

"Lord God, we thank you for the blessings you have given us this day and every day. We trust in you to help our family to do our best in doing the right thing. Dear God, we ask that you please help our son Richie and other children like him. Please help him to talk, make friends, and help him to control his body. We thank you, God, for every day we have together as a family. We pray to you in Jesus' name, Amen."

Before my mom leaves the room, she looks at me and says,

"We must always pray and have faith in our Heavenly Father. Good night, my heart."

I think about God after mom leaves my room. I think about what to pray for. I am eight years old and I have a disability. I don't speak out loud, but my words are always in my head.

I wonder, God, can you hear my non-speaking voice?

God, if you can hear my non-speaking voice, I pray for people to hear me.

I want to tell my mom, dad, brother, and sister how much I love them. I want to thank them for all their help and everything they do for me every day.

God, if you can hear my non-speaking voice, I want to thank my teachers, therapists, doctors, and friends for all the help they have given me.

God, if you can hear my non-speaking voice, I want to control my body. Sometimes I can't control my hands, arms, and legs. It's really hard to do things if I'm always rocking back and forth, flapping my hands, or hitting myself on the head. Sometimes, I look scary to other people and they may not want to be near me. I want to be able to control my body so I can have fun with my family, kids in my class and the friends I hope to make.

God, if you can hear my non-speaking voice, I want to make friends. I want to tell them my name and talk about things I like doing. I want to ask them their name and learn about what they like to do. I want to play games with my family and friends. I want to share my toys and learn about the toys and games that other kids like to play.

God, if you can hear my non-speaking voice, I want to learn new things. I want to tell people how much I know. My teachers sometimes teach me things I already know like the alphabet or counting to ten. Sometimes, I get so bored and mad in class that I hit myself or other people around me. I don't want to do it, but I can't help it. I want to tell them that I can learn new and different things. I know it's not easy for them either, please help them too, God.

God, if you can hear my non-speaking voice, I want to go to church with my family. I want to sing songs and read the bible. I want to learn more about you and all the things you did for us because my mom says you love us.

God, if you can hear my nonspeaking voice, I want to be able to do all these things so I can help other kids like me.

I can tell kids without disabilities how to be nice and friendly to kids like me.

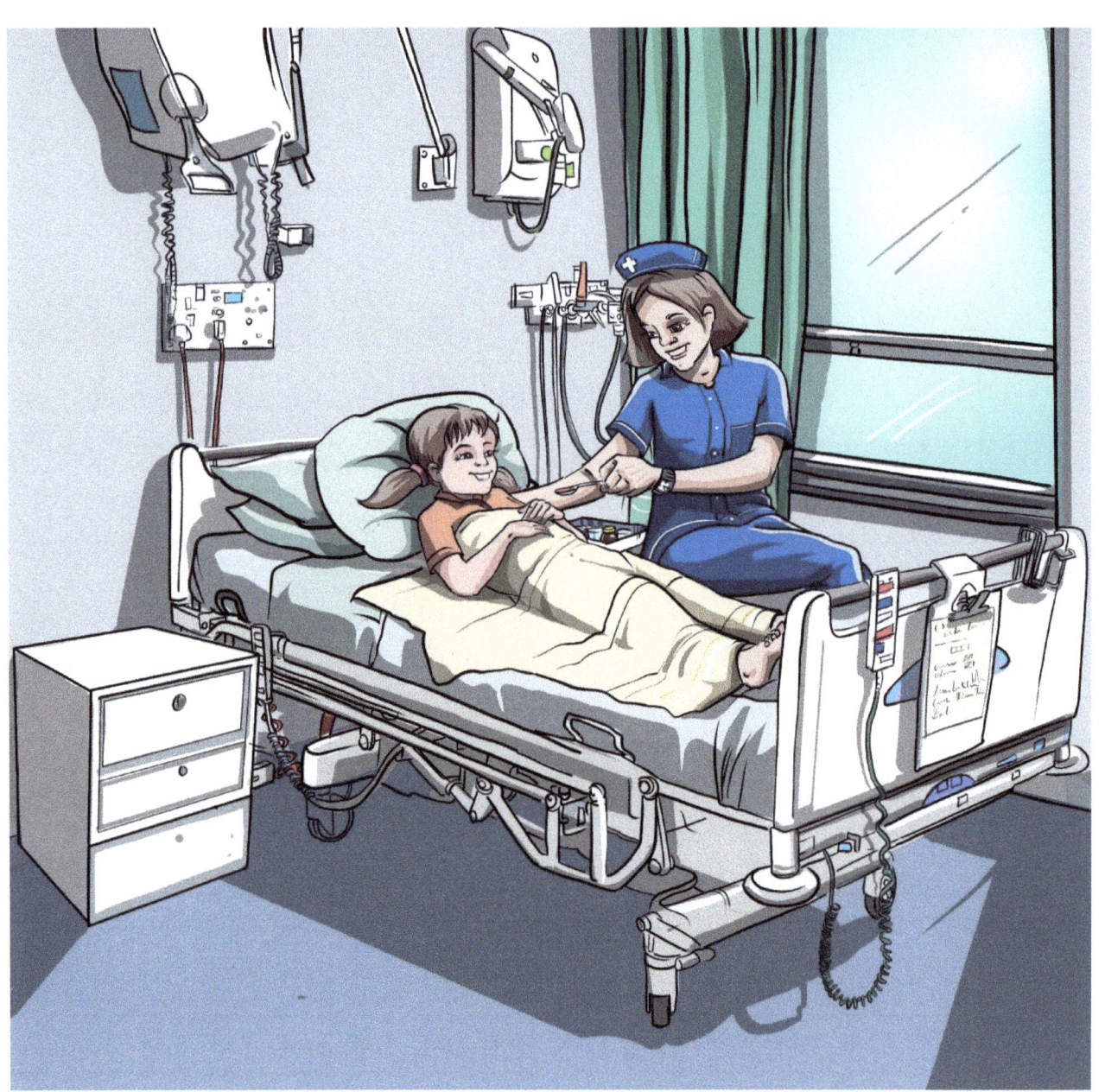

God, if you can hear my non-speaking voice, I know you're busy. I know that there are many other kids who need your help too. Some kids need you more than I do. I pray that you help all kids with and without special needs who need you.

God, I know you may not give me a speaking voice right now. My mom says that you hear all prayers, but may not answer them right away. Until then, would you please help me find a way to get everyone to understand me better?

I love you God, and I thank you for the family, friends, teachers, and life you gave me.

I pray to you in Jesus' name, Amen.

Tips for Maintaining Faith-Based Practices

It is often challenging for special needs families to begin and maintain a life-of faith-based practices, such as daily prayer, attending church services, or participating in faith-based activities. Many situations are unique to each family and their needs. It's not always easy to attend a service, but here are some ideas that we tried and may help your family.

Begin nightly prayers with your child or as a family.

Children with special needs learn with both modeling and repetition. It may take a lot of work and a long time for them to participate in their individual way. But in time they will look forward to praying with you as it becomes part of their routine. I taught my son the Lord's Prayer by breaking it down verse by verse. I would say, "Our Father Who Art in Heaven," and wait for him to repeat it. After he did, we went on to the next verse, "Hallowed be thy name," and so on. Today, he recites it independently with very little prompting, but he memorized it and now knows he can pray whenever he wants to.

Watch the Church service online together as a family.

There are many churches that live stream and record their weekly service and activities on their websites. Pick a time that works best with your family's schedule and routine. It's a great way to practice going to church and to know what to expect when we are ready to attend. I now listen to faith-based podcasts and different sermons in the car on my way to work.

Do Some Research online for Special Needs Ministries in your neighborhood.

Many faith-based communities and churches are very conscious of their outreach. Some are expanding their efforts by trying different ways to make sure God's word reaches everyone. There may be a special needs ministry near you!

One of the most common first prayer ever learned and most recited is The Lord's Prayer:

The Lord's Prayer
Our Father, who Art in Heaven
Hallowed be thy name.
Thy kingdom come, thy will be done
On earth as it is in heaven.
Give us this day, Our daily bread,
And forgive us our trespasses,
As we forgive those who trespassed
Against us. And Lead us not into
Temptation, but deliver us from evil,

Amen.

There is no wrong way to pray as our Heavenly Lord hears us all. God is always waiting for us to welcome Him and love Him. He wants us to trust in Him and ask for help if and when we need it. It is never too late to develop a loving relationship with God.

About the Author

 Christine is a special-needs, storytelling mom who is an inclusion and special needs advocate. Being a special needs parent-led advocate, Christine chose to dedicate her life to serving as an advocate for individuals and families of children with disabilities. Christine is a believer in creating inclusive communities, increasing student achievement with meaningful parent involvement practices, and helping parents be well-informed advocates for their children. Christine believes everyone should have the ability and access to practice their faith with their community's support.

Christine is the creator of www.SensoryFriends.com; a site with resources and a special needs directory dedicated to helping families become inclusion advocates. She has served as a Board and Committee member of the Autism Society of Florida, NCLB (No Child Left Behind), ECTAC (East Coast Technical Assistance Center), Committee of Practitioners for ESSA (Every Student Succeeds Act) and Florida PIRC (Parent Involvement Resource Center), Special Advisory Committee for The Florida Association for Positive Behavior Support, The Home and Community Positive Behavior Support, several local Parent Support Groups, School and ESE (Exceptional Student Education), and Advisory Councils of several School Districts in the state of Florida.

Christine served as a Governor-appointed member of the Florida Rehabilitation Council (charged with collaborating with Vocational Rehabilitation in helping individuals with disabilities obtain and maintain gainful employment). Christine continues to help parents and self-advocates navigate the special education process and inclusion practices.

www.ingramcontent.com/pod-product-compliance
Lightning Source LLC
Chambersburg PA
CBHW042030100526
44587CB00029B/4357